TOE TO TOE
WITH ANXIETY

GENE SCHREYER

WestBow
PRESS®
A DIVISION OF THOMAS NELSON
& ZONDERVAN

Copyright © 2018 Gene Schreyer.

All rights reserved. No part of this book may be used or reproduced by any means, graphic, electronic, or mechanical, including photocopying, recording, taping or by any information storage retrieval system without the written permission of the author except in the case of brief quotations embodied in critical articles and reviews.

Scripture taken from the King James Version of the Bible.

WestBow Press books may be ordered through booksellers or by contacting:

WestBow Press
A Division of Thomas Nelson & Zondervan
1663 Liberty Drive
Bloomington, IN 47403
www.westbowpress.com
1 (866) 928-1240

Because of the dynamic nature of the Internet, any web addresses or links contained in this book may have changed since publication and may no longer be valid. The views expressed in this work are solely those of the author and do not necessarily reflect the views of the publisher, and the publisher hereby disclaims any responsibility for them.

Any people depicted in stock imagery provided by Getty Images are models, and such images are being used for illustrative purposes only.
Certain stock imagery © Getty Images.

ISBN: 978-1-9736-3278-8 (sc)
ISBN: 978-1-9736-3279-5 (e)

Library of Congress Control Number: 2018907705

Print information available on the last page.

WestBow Press rev. date: 07/05/2018

CONTENTS

Synopsis vii
Prologue ix

Chapter 1   Big W 1
Chapter 2   Mr. Nice Guy 5
Chapter 3   Ego Man 19
Chapter 4   When God Is in Your Corner 27

What God Says about Anxiety 33

SYNOPSIS

For me, there were three major opponents that always knocked me out in the ring of life. After knowing how to slip its punches and counter its jabs, you too can overcome anxiety in four rounds, and then you knock it out in the first round yourself. I'll briefly introduce you to these three brutes.

1. Big W

This guy was the toughest one for me to beat personally. "What if?" was his biggest punch—a powerful right hand that crippled me before I even made a move. This question is what we ask ourselves before doing something out of our comfort zone.

2. Mr. Nice Guy

Don't be fooled by his name—this guy isn't nice by any imagination! When we worry about what others think about us and how they perceive us, we pull our punches in life. In other words, we don't do what we are able to do and should do. It is a deceptive mindset based in fear of acceptance and confrontation. I found that this guy will uppercut you with a big smile on his face.

3. Ego Man, aka Pretty Boy

His name is Ego. He's fast and is a total showman, always striving to look on top. He's similar to the fighting style of Mr. Nice Guy, but he uses his mouth as his greatest weapon. His objective is to heckle you into quitting. His opponents always lose from being taunted from missed punches; they eventually lose the courage to come after him altogether. I have found that what prevents us from moving forward in the ring of life is the fear of failing, or rather looking bad if we should fail.

PROLOGUE

Imagine being in a high school locker room a few minutes before kickoff. You're sitting on a bench and tying the laces of your cleats. You listen and feel the vibrations of drums and electric guitars ricochet off the concrete floors and through your body. With each breath, you increasingly notice the stale, warm air around you. This isn't a home game, and so your senses automatically try to analyze the hundreds of different odors your nose is picking up. Sweat, obviously. Cow manure (this is in the country, so not out of place). Hydraulic fluid and axle grease, potatoes, leather, dirt, and at least three different body sprays. The dusty metal from the locker room cabinets. The tile floor, and each of your teammates' unique smell. You couldn't care less about the odors, but your instincts are hard-wired to notice them intently.

As you look around, you can't help but feel the atmosphere in the air as your teammates adjust their shoulder pads and tighten their straps. Therefore, you begin to analyze each person to see what they're contributing to the ambiance of the room. Some look totally relaxed and confident, as if they're not getting ready to go out and play but are showing up to win, like it was already written down in history. Others look very tense. You can see it in their eyes: it's not fear but uncertainty.

"There it is," you tell yourself. "That's where this vibe is coming from."

The rest are careless and free-hearted. Some are telling jokes, and others look bored, as if this event means very little.

With this data you just gathered, you then compare yourself to the others around you. The first thing you notice is that you are terrified, and after this happens, you realize you are the only one in this room who feels like this. The only one. Your brain automatically tries to give you reasons for this, as if to somehow fan out this inferno wave of panic with logic. It doesn't take long. You remember making an embarrassing mistake on the field the previous week. Though no one said anything, you know everybody thought you were stupid. You think of another reason. You realize that you're far from the fitness level of everybody else. So on the field, you know you will burn out sometime during the game and stumble on the field. Everybody will think you are a loser while you lie on the grass hyperventilating, your hometown watches you, and your rivals stand above you and mock you. You see this happening right before your eyes.

Then it happens: your heart begins to beat wildly, so hard you can see each pump pushing out of your chest. You take a deep breath but feel no air entering your lungs. Therefore you inhale even deeper and more frequent. Still, you feel like you're deprived of oxygen. Your fingers, and then all the way down your forearm, fall asleep and throb as if hundreds of needles are stabbing them. After that, the floor suddenly slants to a forty-five-degree angle, and everything you see sways back and forth, in and out of range. You look around and slightly tilt your head to match what you perceive is horizontal, yet the gravitational pull is telling your brain that up and down are on a sloped angle. This frightens you, and so you immediately stand up. However, you can't. Your body now feels as if you weigh more then you can ever attempt to deadlift. You turn the trunk of your waist so you can use both arms to press against the bench. Then as you use your arms for support, you use all the strength of your legs, which are quivering under the enormous weight, to slowly get onto your feet. When you finally stand up, you feel an overwhelming force that wants to pull you straight backward. To overcome this, you lean forward. Realizing that you cannot stand much longer with the overpowering weight and angled floor and dizziness, you head to a bench ahead of you. As you walk toward the bench, your eyes widen because you can't judge the distance; everything becomes larger and smaller in view. As you walk on the wall, which was originally the floor, you pray you can make it to the bench without collapsing. When your shin touches the bench in front of you, your body drops like a fallen bridge as you reach out your arms to take hold.

"Line up!"

Just then, you hear your coach bellow that command, which suddenly grips you with fear.

"Oh, man," you tell yourself. "What am I going to do? I'm not ready!"

Other players quickly grab their helmets and line up two by two, facing the door. Somehow, perhaps out of fear of humiliation, you muster the strength to get up again—which is no easier then the first time. You grab your helmet and race behind the back of the line, trying to appear as if nothing is happening. The ground is still slanted, your teammates in front of you are swaying in and out of focus, and the door opens. With a loud cry, your team marches out of the door, pounding their sides in unison like a beating drum. The only comfort in all this is the encouraging pat of your coach's hand against your helmet as you march into the blinding light of the sun.

If you can imagine this, you've just entered my world of fear and anxiety attacks, which consumed my life for decades. All the sensations I experienced above was an actual event during a high school football game. However, this didn't happen only on that day. It was every game, every practice, and every day I stepped outside the comfort of my home.

For most people, having some level of fear or anxiety of failure or looking bad in front of others before a public speech, an important game, or a major deal in progress that would benefit one's career, has happened at least once in their lifetime. For some, however, fear or anxiety is a gross understatement. It is terror, and it rules over their lives like an evil dictator, preventing them from living. Many who live under it cannot say they really live at all, but merely exist.

If you suffer from constant fear, anxiety attacks, and phobias of any kind that prevent you from living a normal life, then this book was written for you, and it comes from someone who knows what it's like to live that way. If you are a teacher, a pastor or minister, a coach, a family member, or a friend who knows somebody struggling, I greatly encourage you to read this so that you can hopefully get a glimpse into what life in this prison looks like.

Before I go any further, I have to address that without the Lord Jesus Christ, I could not have overcome this. You will see in my story that God placed everything I needed at the right time and place, which gave me the tools to finally step outside the prison I was in, all while drawing me closer to him. It was a long and difficult journey, but without the need of any medication whatsoever. Now, God might use medication for your recovery. However, I can say for myself that I can't give one tiny piece of credit to pills. My point is this: don't take the easier route and start popping pills to cure your anxiety, specifically if it's in the category of a phobia. It *will not* solve the heart of the issue! Even if you have a chemical imbalance such as a serotonin deficiency and require medication, you still want to help yourself as much as possible without them. I'm not anti-medication; I'm simply saying too many people rely wholeheartedly on them without taking on any responsibility or being willing to work hard and adopt healthy risks to better themselves (emphasis on *healthy* risks; I'll explain that later on). More important, God created us to fellowship with him. Do not use medication, drugs, alcohol, or any means as a way to leave Him out when you're having anxiety, when he himself wants to comfort you.

With that said, let me share my knowledge and experience about panic attacks, phobias, and general anxiety, along with truths in God's Word that deal with these very issues.

CHAPTER 1

Big W

Countering the "What If?" Question

"hat if?" Two small but powerful words that stop you in your tracks as if you're on the receiving end of George Foreman's fist. While growing up with anxiety over anything that stretched my circle of comfort, I never grasped how much this question impacted me directly until I learned how to see it and then later slip this punch of a question. I'd never seen this punch coming, which was why I kept hitting the canvas. Why look at it, though? After all, it was just a simple question in my head, right? I never took notice of it because it sounded reasonable and logical to ask this question. It was as simple as calculating whether I could jump over a mud puddle or should walk around it. *No big deal*, I thought.

When my caseworker would come to my home (at that time, my comfort zone had shrunk to the confines of my house), she would try to get me to take on a healthy risk. A healthy risk is doing something that is out of your comfort zone but is not self-harming. For example, if you fear public speaking, you volunteer to read in front of a group of kids, or you do next week's business presentation. I remember during one session, she asked me to take on such a challenge, and I insisted it would cause me to potentially die in fear.

As I explained my reasons, she interrupted me. "Gene," she said with a smile, "do you know what you keep saying?"

"Um, no. What?" I answered.

"You keep saying, 'What if?'"

"'What if?'" I said.

"Yeah. 'What if this?' and 'What if that?' That is your biggest problem. You need to stop asking yourself, 'What if?'"

This was a huge eye-opener for me. Before that, I had never realized how much I was asking myself that question.

Immediately after that session, I began thinking about all the issues that I had. I connected the dots on my thinking pattern and my anxiety. Here's an example I had in regard to my phobia about driving during traffic. It had gotten so bad that I never drove anywhere past 9:00 a.m., when the traffic became heavy. When I had to for work, I got out of the car soaked with sweat, my arms numb and tingling. I was completely out of energy and was exhausted before I even started work!

Here's what I'd ask:

> "*What if* I crash? I can't afford to fix anything."

> "*What if* I stall on a red light, and an angry driver starts yelling at me?"

> "*What if* there's construction, and I don't know where to go?"

> "*What if* I make a wrong turn, and those in the car with me think I'm stupid?"

I will get to the point of all this, because I can spend too much time listing all my "What if?" questions regarding all the phobias I had. The point is that when Big W throws this question at you, it's not to get you to make an informed decision about something worth thinking about. It's to list reasons why you shouldn't do it.

When I asked myself this question, I realized I wasn't asking in order to prepare myself for that possible scenario, but to give me a reason to throw in the towel and simply not attempt it. Another problem with this question is that "What if?" has so much weight that it gets treated as "What will?" In other words, it becomes a prophetical way of thinking without any resolve to prepare for it. The "What if I stall on a red light?" becomes "If I drive, *I will* stall on a red light."

So how do you slip this question, and how do you turn off this question when it's screaming in your head? Well, carrying on the theme, you do not want to catch and parry this punch. You want to slip it. When I took on my fear of driving and headed toward the car, my stomach filled with butterflies, and my ears were attentive to the sounds of cars whizzing past my driveway. The what-ifs swung at me in all directions. Now when the questions entered my mind, I didn't catch them and take the time to analyze them (catch and parry). I simply redirected my thoughts (slipped the punch entirely) and continued toward the car. At first it was very difficult for me to slip every question, but trust me: it gets easier as you keep making a habit to redirect your thoughts that seem to be going against the very fabric of survival instincts. However, if you keep doing it, it becomes a habit, and one day the screaming voices become whispers.

I remember one day, after driving in the middle of rush hour and thanking God, I thought, *Wow! Last year I could never do this and be so relaxed!* It was so gratifying to climb a hill that was once a dreadful mountain.

"But *what if* one day really becomes *what did?*" If you're now thinking this, I metaphorically slap you with brotherly love because you just got punched again. Remember to slip the punches entirely—don't catch and parry those questions.

If you are not saved or not right with God, I recommend skipping to the last chapter, because it is in the Lord Jesus Christ you can trust everything in life. When you're fighting Big W—whether a fear of driving, speaking in public, being in crowds, or anything else—all you have to do is slip its one question, and you *will* be able to knock it out!

CHAPTER 2

Mr. Nice Guy

Pulling Your Punches and People Pleasing

r. Nice Guy is a man who is tall, has a calm and friendly voice, has wavy blond hair, and has a smile from ear to ear, revealing a perfect set of whitened teeth. In this chapter, we're going to go over how to knock this guy's teeth out, because he is a wolf in sheep's clothing. When you're in the ring with him, you'll move around and quickly notice that he can't react fast enough to your punches. Soon you land a good shot to his strong butt chin, which drops him on his knees. The audience is dominated with his fans, and so the theater echoes with boos and gasps.

Before the count, he gets up and looks at you with his big, blue eyes while holding his chin. "Take it easy, eh, buddy?" he says as you bump gloves. "We're all just having fun here."

Now you feel bad, and so you start going easy on him, slowing your punches and throwing with less power. Every time he slips your punches, the audience cheers, and now surprisingly you start hearing more cheers for you than you did before. The round is going well, and you feel great, thinking he was right about you. You've gained more of the crowd by pulling back, and you know you'll have to win by landing a few more points than he does. *Just enjoy the ride*, you think.

Suddenly and without warning, he springs out and throws machine-gun punches with lightning speed, repeatedly landing shots square on your chin. Then he finishes by lunging in with a hook to your liver. It happened all too fast, and now you are on the canvas.

In a daze and in pain, you hear the crowd start roaring as Mr. Nice Guy has his arms raised in the air. All the fans who were cheering for you are now all for Mr. Nice Guy. In the end, you lost.

This analogy may be extreme, but that is exactly what happens when we fail to do what is right or to be open and honest in a situation where we fear losing the praise or acceptance of others. We begin by pulling our punches (not giving our best). Those of us who are saved through Jesus Christ can start pulling our punches by not doing or saying things that God wants us to do or say from this same type of fear.

In the end, people pleasing will always lead us to getting beat up on the inside. Before I dig into this, I want to point out that in my lifetime, I have met many people who have said they struggle with low self-esteem and anxiety, but they were always complaining because they did something for somebody, making sure the world recognized and gave them praise for something they did because they were "always thinking of others first." These same people have no problem expressing any displeasure they may have, making a public scene. This includes men, women, and children who can't understand economics, yet they know that the customer service is too slow, the prices are too high, or their cheese isn't properly melted. Their public outcry is as passionate as a flock of seagulls begging for french fries. Well, I have to say that there is that similar adrenaline response due to anger and frustration when someone doesn't act or a circumstance doesn't happen to one's liking. Yes, they start shaking, their heart rates go up, they sweat, and they have difficulty talking as they would during a panic attack. But who I'm talking about here are those who have those feelings and cannot express them at all in a healthy, beneficial way. If they express their true feelings with any level of honesty, the other person might disapprove. Therefore they hold it in and lie about it. True people pleasers are dependent on the positive emotions, approval, and feedback of others, regardless of how they themselves are feeling.

For me, this was another large opponent who kept knocking me down for most of my life as I grew up. I suffered many years with anxiety and hated going out in public around people, but I thought it was because of my fear of harm from being outside. Then I read the book *When Panic Attacks* by David D. Burns. I remember praying in the library one day (one of the few places I actually enjoyed going to in my agoraphobic years) that the Lord would lead me to some material that would help me get over my consuming fears. Like a bright yellow sign, I then saw the title of this book staring straight at me on the shelf, and I immediately picked it up. It was here that I made a connection with my anxiety when I was around people. While reading it, I realized that fear of harm was not the total cause of my anxiety; I also had a terrible fear of conflict and disapproval of others. When someone put me in a situation I didn't like at school or work, or said something that I didn't agree with, I would lock up and start getting dizzy. After years of this happening, I ended up fearing talking to people at all due to my physical responses, and therefore I came to the conclusion that it was people alone that caused me to avoid them all together. To me, people equaled danger.

Until I explored this area, I never realized how the fear of conflict or disapproval can feel like danger itself. Once I made the connection, I still struggled a long time with people because for me, I couldn't bear the negative feelings I felt when someone contradicted my opinions or I didn't live up to someone's expectations. *Why?* I asked myself, *Why do I need people's approval? Why am I afraid to hear someone's negative feedback? Why can't I be honest about this situation?* I want to be very careful here because in this day and age, self-love is being grossly exaggerated beyond a Godly sense of the word. That being said, the reason why I kept being beat in this area is because I was dependent on others' approval for my own sense of worth or wellness; I was codependent.

As I grew up, I formed an opinion on how I viewed myself compared to those around me. To be succinct, I felt beneath most every person I met. Due to the fact that I was convinced I was beneath everybody else, whenever I did something nice for someone, I would get a pat on the back and a compliment and would instantly feel good about myself. This validation from them was intoxicating, and it was then that I eventually became a people pleaser. During the times of "selfless" acts of service, I no longer felt low because I was getting positive feedback. When I missed someone's mark and disappointed anyone who meant a grain of salt to me, I would feel that disappointment and instantly fall back to feeling like I was no good. I was convinced that I was at the bottom of the social ranks of men, and as hard as I tried to talk myself into feeling better, I could not shake how I truly felt about myself. Whenever somebody else complimented me, that meant something.

You can see where this is going. Without realizing it, I had adopted this behavioral way of thinking for so long to the point where I didn't even realize my true motives for my actions until years later, when my body had just enough of being nice. After years of this way of living, the stress eventually erupted from years of not saying no when I really couldn't, being honest when I didn't want to, and expressing myself when someone crossed the line—even if it meant that person would not approve or like me. All that that pent-up stress was held inside in sacrifice to the altar of personal acceptance, apart from the acceptance I could have freely had through Jesus Christ. I want to point out here that this way of living is idolatry because it is meeting a need apart from God. Mr. Nice Guy looks very good on the outside. He is always on the front pages, holding an autographed baby in his arms or holding a bowl of soup in the shelter for the homeless. On the inside, however, he is manipulating the crowd for his own personal agenda and is entirely selfish. "More fans, more money" is his motto.

Out of nowhere one day, my body had simply had enough of this and began expressing what was happening in my mind through panic attacks. You see, panic attacks are not merely responses to fear alone. They're a means of releasing built-up stress that you are either afraid or unwilling to address and release. When this happens, your body builds up with pressure and then finally erupts like a volcano because it wants to purge what is mentally harming you. Your body responds to mental stress just as it does to physical stress. A person who has a terrible fear of butterflies will produce the same kind of physical responses as someone who has just seen a loose tiger on the street. When this happens in either case, the body goes into a phase called the fight-or-flight response. When you perceive a threat, your body gears up to either fight (express it) or flight (run away). The butterfly is harmless, but because the person's perception of it is frightening and therefore stressful, the body will treat it as a serious problem.

The biggest physical problem with people pleasing is that because being afraid of the negative conflations or lack of approval if one is honest to another or says "no" to a personal favor, they don't let their bodies release this stress as they go along with it. If left untreated, this will cause them to become anxious, and anxiety attacks won't be far off in the future. In a biblical sense, a person who suffers anxiety even around the church family might be one who does every favor or every request asked regardless of one own circumstances, or is never honest to someone about a crossed personal boundary or offense.

Those who do this are deceiving themselves. They may think they are being selfless or turning the cheek when actually, under the spiritual microscope, the majority of their motives is for their own edification through the need of praise and validation through others. They don't express any true emotion to an offence or crossed boundary in order to reconcile; it's not because they're overlooking the offence as in Proverbs 19:11, but because their need of validation is more important than saying anything. They don't say no to a request, and it's not because they have the desire to serve God or to honestly help. Saying no might disappoint others, and so they fear they might get a negative response—in other words, cutting down their sense of worth. Those like me who practiced this type of behavior think they are helping themselves, but actually they've just doubled the damage.

To dig deeper, God's Word says we as Christians should express (with love of course) our feelings to another about an offense (Matthew 18:15.)

Before you take the action of not taking any action, or in the case of the times you say yes in taking action, examine your motives and remember this verse: "All the ways of a man are clean in his own eyes; but the Lord weigheth the spirits" (Proverbs 16:2). The Lord knows and weighs your true motives for doing good, so make sure you're honest with yourself.

So How Do I Beat Mr. Nice Guy?

Okay, now that I addressed the strategy and deception of Mr. Nice Guy, I will tell you how you can beat him so that you can become victorious in the ring of life and deal with people pleasing.

First: Fix the perception of yourself first.

This is crucial because it is very hard to stand in contradiction with your peers, or people in general, when you feel low self-worth and are in need of validation. Here's what I had to realize: stop basing your worth on the success of your own circumstances; rather base it on what you are doing in those circumstances. Whether you are losing, poor, sick, weak, or lacking in skill or intelligence, what defines you as a person is what you are doing in those circumstances. Whenever I was around those who I envisioned as having it better than I did (better genetics, money, intelligence, etc.), I would look at myself to compare and then feel inferior. Therefore it was easier for me to get in the habit of tucking my tail between my legs around those kinds of people. This thinking is a fallacy because over the years, I have seen others who were in the exact set of circumstances (or worse) as I was, and they ended up doing well or even going beyond in success.

I looked down on myself for growing up poor, only to read about 'great men who grew up poorer then I was. I looked down on myself for not having the physical ability as another, only to see someone who grew up with greater physical impairments then I have and far excelled me in the world of fitness. One man named Mikey, whom I had the pleasure of meeting at Empowering Punch, has type two diabetes and is mostly deaf, yet he is a successful soccer coach and is a great personal trainer there. Despite his body's inability to control blood sugar, he is lean and in superior shape. He helps hundreds of people get in shape themselves and become successful in the world of sports. Despite his need for a hearing aid, he can call out punching combos and commands during a music-blaring, packed class in the exact fashion and skill as the rest of the trainers.

When you meet these kinds of people, you feel that they don't let their identities be defined by what they have or don't have. They simply work hard, focus on their goals, and don't spend time looking at everyone else. It's an amazing quality that everyone can have. My point is the key way to stop basing your worth on your circumstances is to stop looking at the circumstances of everyone else. This may seem obviously simple, but it's the practice of doing this that is difficult to do.

Second: Don't let other people's opinions about yourself dictate your security and who you are.

This sounds simple, but again it's hard to overcome and to practice. I can tell you that every year I had social anxiety and panic attacks, my feelings of security rested on the feedback and opinions of other people. When I talk about security, I mean a sense of overall peace. I could express an idea that I was 100 percent sure of, but if the other party disagreed or flat out didn't like it, then I felt fear, as if I was in danger somehow. This caused me to quickly change my opinion or agree on that person's side of the issue so that I would feel safe again.

When I was living in the confines of my house and feeling sorry about myself, I would watch interviews and documentaries (I had a lot of time on my hands) of those who I felt had brave personality and could stand boldly in the fire of criticism--a quality that I wanted to have. Some of these people were heckled and booed, but mostly they were confronted by other people's disagreements. In other words, people were trying to get them to change an opinion in order to please their own.

As I listened to them speak, I realized the common theme they all had was that they knew who they were and what they stood for. Because of this, they did not care what others thought of them because their identities were not in the hands of others. As you can see, if you leave your identity to the mercy of others' approval, how can you ever escape people pleasing? In my experience, you can't. The first thing that I had to realize in doing this was learn that it is okay to be in contradiction to someone else. It is okay for someone to say, "I disagree with you." When that feeling of anxiety came upon me during those recovering moments of "I disagree," I had to tell myself, *It's okay, Gene. You're okay*. It was hard to pull away from this pattern of thinking because doing so made me feel like a penguin leaving the safety of the waddle (group) and jumping into the ocean among a pod of orcas. As I practiced this, however, the feelings themselves became easier to deal with.

I remember during a small church service, a woman said, "I don't agree with you there," to my good friend and mentor, Matt, during his message.

He looked at her, and smiled with a friendly face and said, "It's okay if you don't agree with me." I sat there and was amazed. The world didn't end. He didn't cry or get really red and blush in shame. I observed this unprecedented event (in my circle, anyway) and was amazed that her statement didn't move him at all. Why was that? It was her opinion, and that's okay because his opinion and who he is was not affected by it. Those things were not given into her hand but his identity, and what he said was based on his relationship in Christ and the Word of God. When I stopped basing my feelings of security on other people's perceptions or opinions of me, I slowly learned who I am, what I'm about, and what I stand for. The fear, anxiety, and uncertainty of many things vanished.

Third: Work at your own pace, no one else's.

In my own story, two events happened in the later years of my life that further helped me defeat Mr. Nice Guy. The first was when I was at work at a tire and lube shop. I had full-blown agoraphobia and social anxiety back then, so simply clocking in at work after a frightening drive left me physically drained. While working there, I remember my co-workers noticing my trembling hands as I punched in the car's data on the screen; my blood sugar was constantly low from the adrenalin. No matter how much I tried to hide it, it was always visible. Nevertheless, I remember talking to a coworker, whom I'll call Tony. While he worked at this job, I could see that he always worked hard, yet he never rushed and was always calm and collective; he was never anxious. We were on the subject of rushing to keep the line of cars flowing at the manager's level of acceptance. I remember him telling me something that always stuck with me. I told him how I was anxious because I couldn't be faster. He looked at me and said, "You can only work at your own pace, Gene, no one else's."

Then he told me how a manager once told him he wasn't working fast enough and to speed up. "I told him, 'I work at my own pace, sir.' I'm sorry it isn't yours.'"

That hit me. Was he deliberately being slow? No, but he expressed that he worked at a pace where he could best do his job. He did not fret because someone else didn't like it. Back then, I would have rushed in order to please my boss, which would have increased my anxiety. I see this everywhere, and in this world of fast food and fast service, I see workers coming to me suffering from panic attacks, high blood pressure, and other health problems due to this.

Rushing should be used for emergencies. If you're constantly in a rush, you're putting a huge tax on your adrenal glands, which will cause anxiety, panic attacks, adrenal fatigue, and other harm to your body. Most jobs these days (that pay minimum wage, at least) are staffed to a bare minimum, which means extra job duties performed in the same expected amount of time. If you are a good worker, you can bet that these places will not be in a rush to hire more help if you're able to do it alone, and so you need to be able to handle this stress so that you can be a dependable employee. Working fast doesn't mean you are rushing, but if you're rushing, you're not working fast. In order to be fast, you have to rush, which means you are going beyond what you can do proficiently.

How can you tell? Your stress level. When I returned to work, I found myself working alone most of the time, and there was a mountain of things to do. It was expected that I finished at the same time as if I was working with a full staff. Well, I worked at the same pace as if we were fully staffed. When asked me to do something faster, I acknowledged with a "yes sir or ma'am" and continued working at the pace I knew I was capable, of without causing my adrenalin to spike.

Some of you may ask, "Well, what about Colossians 3: 22? 'Servants, obey in all things your masters according to the flesh.' So by not working faster (rushing), am I not being a good employee?"

I'm glad you asked. Read carefully: "not with eye service, as …" What? "Men-pleasers; but in singleness of heart, fearing God."

Is your motivation to rush to please your boss, or to please God out of a willing heart? Also read verse 23: "and, whatsoever ye do, do it heartily as to the Lord, and not unto men."

In this context, rushing is service rendered out of stress and obligation in order to please men. If you are working out of love and devotion toward God, you will not be rushing, and stress will not be in the equation. See the difference? A great example of fast hard labor due to the devotion to God, rather than the slavery of men pleasing, is the reconstruction of the wall of Jerusalem in Nehemiah chapters 1–7.

The second story is while talking to Paul Scianna (aka the Perfect Storm), the owner and trainer at Empowering Punch. I was getting down on myself because I felt I lacked the same ability as my classmates.

"Gene, you can only do you," he said. "Forget about everyone else. You want to be the best version of yourself." That bit of advice hit home, and from then on I had no problem being in the ring with anyone else, regardless of skills. If you want to be a basketball player, you will never be Kobe Bryant. If you want to be an evangelist, you will never be Billy Graham. If you want to be a boxer, you will never be George Foreman. You will always be you, and God has only made one you. Be the best version of you. Don't spend life trying to be someone else.

If you work on applying these simple things, you can bring Mr. Nice Guy down to the canvas, and you'll be free from his deceiving tactics and tricks so that you can be the best version of yourself.

CHAPTER 3

Ego Man

Leaving Your Ego Behind in Order to Go Forward

go Man. Everybody knows when he's around because he is the center of attention. He's a loudmouthed showman who, before the fight the next day, arrives with an ensemble of his loyal friends to heckle you at your favorite coffee shop.

"Hey, you!" he shouts. You don't look at him but sit at the table, minding your own business. Then you start to feel the vibrations of strong footsteps coming closer to your table.

"Hey, boy."

Suddenly your shoulders are shoved forward, sending hot coffee and whipped cream up your nostrils.

"Look at you." He chuckles with an obnoxious laugh so everyone in the room can hear. "Jelly arms, man. You can't even hold your coffee!" Now everyone in the room recognizes you, as you wipe your face. All of his friends are laughing, and even some of the customers are trying to conceal their smirks. You're alone, but the shop's manager sees the commotion and starts to walk toward your table.

"Let's go guys," said Big E as he is about to be warned to leave. "Noodle boy needs some rest before I cream him again tomorrow." As his friends follow behind him and give one more insult before they exited, the manger puts his hands on your shoulder.

"Son," he says, "I wouldn't blame ya for skipping town. He's even more obnoxious when he wins."

This scenario is played out in all our lives when we have something we want accomplished but our ego steps in to heckle us. This may seem like the opposite of truth because ego is generally an inflated sense of self-confidence. However, if your ego is anything like Ego Man, then failing to look good—or rather, looking bad in front of others—is a terribly fearful opponent, so much so that you end up skipping town before the fight. In other words, your own ego prevents you from taking on a challenge because of fear.

People suffering from performance anxiety like I did may seem like they are far from having an ego problem, but actually it may be the direct result of it. For example, when I played football in high school, I knew nothing about the sport. I hadn't watched football or picked up a book about it, and so when I was in practice, all I saw during plays was a blur of helmets running in all directions like marbles being poured onto the floor. I played on defense and so was always confused, because we'd be on the field for four plays, then sometimes six plays, then five plays the next time. I can laugh now, but I did some goofy things on the field because I did not know what I was doing. All I knew was to tackle the guy with the ball, and that was it. Nonetheless, my anxiety quickly intensified into panic attacks before each game and practice. Soon I began skipping practice because I would get the panic attacks before school ended.

Years later, I reflected on my football days and on my teammates and coaches, and I realized an astonishing thing. My teammates and coaches were not the reason for my panic attacks at all. In fact, I had the best teammates anyone could ever have. They saw all my mistakes and yet never failed to cheer for me for when I did something well. After one game, they all cheered for me in unison, symbolically handing me the game ball. I missed a lot of practice, yet never was I told to quit the team. I remember once I was so tired that I tripped on a speed ladder, falling over a teammate in front of me and entangling my ankles in the rope; it happened in front of some girls who were watching us practice. I once caught a football by my facemask. I couldn't catch a football if it was dangling from a helium balloon. What I remember from events like these is the encouragement from my teammates, Saguache Colorado's Mountain Valley Indians.

My coach, Coach Harrison, saw my fear. He took me aside and taught me the game of football, and he did not send me on the field when he knew I was ill from the panic attacks. I remember after the season, he told me that he always pushed me as far as he knew I could handle it to make me stronger. This may seem backward, but I prayed each game that he wouldn't send me in at all—and ended up playing much more then I imagined! I am convinced that

God used this very thing to show me what he does with me in life. I'd never run since I was a child, and only then if I saw something scary. My leg muscles were not developed. I would run down the field for a ways, and my legs would crumble beneath me, making me fall under my own weight. Like a kid learning to walk, my legs eventually grew stronger to where I could run without collapsing—but then I had to learn how to run properly. My coach then taught me how to do that.

To get to the point in all this, the reason why I had such anxiety (other than the fear of getting hurt, which was minimal due to all the padding) was actually because of my ego. I needed to look good because deep down, looking stupid would reaffirm what I was already telling myself: that I was under par, a loser, or stupid. This fear was so strong that I couldn't tolerate an experience that affirmed this, and so the pressure would erupt into a volcano state of anxiety.

When Ego Man heckled me, I would forfeit fighting him—only to get knocked out later by Big W. I would tell myself that I was a failure, and then later I'd ask myself, "Well, then what if this happens, which would make me feel worse?"

How to Beat Ego Man

Simply put: step in the ring, and he will forfeit to you. How do you muster the courage to do that? Drop your ego, and he will have nothing on you.

Pride is what the world (social media, Hollywood, magazines, etc.) is all about. It's looking good and being on top. In soap operas, a woman wakes up after a month-long coma with perfectly groomed hair, manicured nails, fresh breath, and a set of bleached teeth. If it is a man, his large biceps and six pack are still in peak shape without a hint of atrophy. Reality is bad breath, messy hair, being last place, or looking bad.

To start, ask yourself one question when you want to achieve something but anxiety prevents you from even trying it. Why do you want to do this?

When I signed up for the football team, it was not because I wanted to play football. It was for the sole purpose of attracting the ladies—to look good. I thought that playing football would magically impress the girls while making me tough. Well, when I went out there, I did not look at myself as impressive at all, but rather the opposite. The strategy actually backfired to where I had no confidence to talk to girls. In all honesty, I didn't care for playing football, especially on a nice Saturday morning. When things got tough, I had nothing inside to pull me through. Why? Because playing football was not something I even wanted to do. I told myself I did, but I was lying to myself. I was there for my ego or for the title of football jock.

If you are doing something to impress other people and increase your sense of pride in yourself, expect anxiety—period. If you are doing something because you want to do it, because you believe in its cause, or simply because you love it, then you will be free from unnecessary performance anxiety and added stress caused from pride. As an agoraphobic playing football, I believe God used it to teach me many things, exposing me to healthy challenges and giving me a firm platform to take me to the next level of recovery. However, I was still left with anxiety at the end of the season.

To be succinct, if you are struggling with agoraphobia or social anxiety, you need to find something that you are passionate about and take on that challenge. Whether that's football, baseball, basketball, volunteer work, or soccer, find something that will throw you out of your comfort zone while doing something you really enjoy. If you join something only because it'll make you look good, there's a good chance it will only get you so far in your recovery. As for me, boxing was something I really enjoyed, so much so that looking bad in front of others was evenly matched by my passion for it. Therefore much of my focus was learning to get better. After each time I sparred, my thoughts were analyzing what happened and what I could do to do better next time. I was not focused on how bad I must have looked. As you see from my story, after football, my thoughts were not geared in a drive to be better—they were entirely consumed by my failures. I tell you in those days of football, I felt worse about myself more times than I felt better because of prideful thinking and an unbalanced lack of interest in the sport.

What do I mean by pride? I mean in the worldly sense, as a mentality that one must look or appear at a greater level than someone else in stature. It means to look pleasing in the eyes of others by way of one's own abilities, accomplishments, or personal being. This way of thinking is sinful, and for me it was a major component in my anxiety. This topic is a book in itself but let's look to the best of the best, the king of kings and Lord of lords, the best human being (yet fully God) who has ever and will ever touch this earth: Jesus Christ.

- When he was born, there was no room for him in the inn. He was delivered in a manger. Not in a clean stable like a petting zoo, but a manger or a stall of hay (Luke 2:7)
- During his ministry here on earth, he had no place to live (Matthew 8:20).
- There was nothing in his appearance that attracted people to him except despised and rejected men (Isaiah 53:1–4).
- Jesus "made himself of no reputation, and took upon him the form of a servant, and was made in the likeness of men" (Philippians 2:7–8 KJV).

Do you still think you need to worry about your appearance? Are you any greater? Of those of you reading this who suffer performance or social anxiety, I can tell you that when I threw in the towel and stopped trying to look good (which is exhausting, by the way), my anxiety levels plummeted. It is hard to start, especially when others are heckling you over a mistake or an opinion of yours, or you drudge over a failure.

However! Yes, the exclamation is needed here. I soon realized that when I purposefully did not care about how I looked to others, when those things did happen, they ran over my shoulders like raindrops. I was amazed at the transformation I felt. Not only did others' criticisms or opinions not faze me, but I found myself owning the situations, not shaming from them. Before, I'd taken the negative responses I'd received from others as the gospel truth. Now, darts like those bounce off like a ping pong ball off a lion's nose. If I make a goof, I own it. So what? I'll try again. Soon, an attitude of calmness and boldness grew out of this into a whole new demeanor. This new demeanor, to my surprise, was what I had seen and searched for in others whom I admired. In common parlance, it's called confidence; as I call it, the world is all about pride and prestige, so it's "I'm here to please God, not you, so your opinion of me doesn't matter." It's a working title.

CHAPTER 4

When God Is in Your Corner

As I wrote this book, I rewrote and changed the overall structure of this project quite a few times. The reason was that I wasn't sure how much information would be edifying and needed in order to make the best impact to those reading my story. After a few times of reconstruction, I realized that my goal for this book is to honestly, simply, and succinctly tell you what steps got me out of the house. It was only after addressing these three major opponents that I was able to recover. The rest of any underlying causes of my agoraphobia, social anxiety, or even general anxiety were mere featherweights compared to these issues, and they were all somehow tied in to one or more of the three. I believe the reason is that these three opponents dealt with two things, which is the heart and soul of most anxiety.

> One: exaggerated, overanalyzed (consuming your thoughts with the worst-case scenario), prophetically assumed, or distortion of reality of the situation caused by overthinking

> Two: body manifestation of pent-up stress, or intolerance of a situation via a panic attack, caused by refusing to deal with or leave the situation honestly, mostly due to people pleasing behavior or fear of conflict

As I'm wrapping this up, I want to tell you what was the most important step in my recovery. I've saved the best for last. Without this, I was at a point in my life of chronic anxiety where I wanted to hang up my gloves and step out of the ring of life for good. In the ring of life, when fighting fearful opponents, you can rest on one of three things to the point where you don't have to fight at all if you so choose.

1. Substances like drugs or alcohol, dulling your senses to where you can't feel your opponent's blows.
2. Yourself, by digging deep inside to find that inner strength.
3. God, the one whom your cause of fear is subject and must bow to.

You can pick two of them, but not all three. You can choose one of them, but one of them demands you don't rely on the other two.

Now I admit that though I was saved in Jesus Christ, I still struggled many years with terrible anxiety. I remember one time in church, I left the crowded auditorium, closed myself in the restroom stall, and asked God why I was having such anxiety, especially in church. "Are you even with me?" I asked. It was hard talking to people about Jesus in those days, when I was going through such anxiety. After all, I should have no fear and total peace, right?

I remember when I was sitting in the cafeteria at a rough school, where I would get bullied now and then. I would read verses in my small Bible like Isaiah 46:3–5, Isaiah 49:15–17, and Isaiah 53:12–13. Though I felt embraced by God, I was still overwhelmed with the symptoms of anxiety. Why? Was God not with me? Did he refuse to give me the peace he promised?

The answer is, Not at all! His peace was always there, but I refused to take it! This simple yet hard-to-practice concept is that God does give us his peace, but we must surrender our fait and rest in him. Imagine someone who is dangling on a rope over a cliff. A man suddenly leans over the precipice with his arms stretched out and yells, "Grab my hand!"

The frightened man writhes, kicking his legs in all directions, and though he sees the hands near him, he continues to scream, holding onto the rope.

"Grab my hand," said the rescuer. "I'll carry you. Just let go!" After a few minutes the man on the rope becomes too weak to hold himself up, but he still refused to grab the hand of his rescuer, and he begins to fall. The rescuer, seeing the man going doing down, grabs the hand himself and pulls him up. Now, though securely in the arms of his rescuer, the man continues to scream, kick, and shake until he is pulled over the edge, never realizing that he was being carried.

This is what I was doing all those years. God was and is carrying me, but when I refuse to let go, I cannot experience the rest and peace he is offering. As I look back, God was with me during all those years of anxiety and frightening situations. Even in certain events, which he allowed to happen, I know and am thankful I was there to see how God was indeed carrying me. All I could do during those times of trouble was be still as he hoisted me on his shoulders like an injured calf.

This is a wonderful truth. If you are one of God's children, though you refuse to let go and needlessly suffer anxiety, the heavenly father himself is holding your hand. The thing I had to realize is that when I was afraid, I thought the reality of my situation was proved by what I was feeling: "I have anxiety, and so God is not with me." Like the frightened man on the rope, we can't blame our anxiety on God. To prove this, look at Peter in Acts 12.

King Herod just killed James, the brother of John, and put Peter in prison, who was escorted by four squads of four soldiers and then later chained between two soldiers (Peter was a high-priority prisoner, for that amount of effort to keep him from escaping). At night, Peter was awaiting trial the next day. Given what happened to James, it's safe to say that Peter was soon to be tried and executed. Most people know this to be Peter's miraculous escape, but what is interesting is what Peter was doing before God rescued him. Peter was sleeping. He was not wide awake with fear, although he must have known what Herod wanted to do to him. He was not only sleeping but was so out that in order to wake him, the angel "smote Peter on the side and raised him up" (Acts 12:7 KJV). In other words, Peter was in deep sleep! This is an example of the rest God gives to his children who trust him. Peter could have refused to let go, staying up all night and anxiously worry about his plight, but he gave his situation to God. It was this man who, by God's instruction, wrote, "Casting all your care [old English anxiety] upon him; for he careth for you" (1 Peter 5:7).

I knew this verse like the back of my hand because it was often quoted to me by pastors and mentors during those years. It wasn't until I obeyed the *casting* part of the verse that I experienced peace firsthand. To cast something away means just that. Don't stew over it, and don't analyze it. Throw it to God because he is caring for you whether or not you trust him.

This brings me to my second point in this. As God's children, we don't just have permission, but we are commanded to not fear! I can spend a lot of time here, but as a person who was a slave to fear, I was so enamored when I came to the realization that God not only suggests but commands me to n to fear. Logically, it seems good to analyze and stew on what terrifies me, because doing so might keep me from experiencing it, or at least I can prepare myself so that if it does happen, it won't traumatize me as much. Drudging over an event I really don't want to go through might somehow keep me from being blindsided by it. The truth is that as an adopted heir of God, it is not my responsibility to worry about myself. Neither is it fitting, because God is my heavenly father. God doesn't want his children to worry. As any parent, he would be hurt over his child not trusting in his protective arms.

If you are not born again, then you are not a child of God, and so you are left to the devices of this world for comfort. I encourage you to ask Jesus into your heart. He paid for your sins, and by his sacrifice in your place, he gave way to where you can be an adopted child of God. I hope this rings out not as a servant but a son or daughter of the one who made us. Let God be in your corner so that when you don't have the strength to fight on, he will step in the ring and fight for you.

WHAT GOD SAYS ABOUT ANXIETY

Important Verses to Commit to Memory
When Dealing with Anxiety

This is a short list of Bible verses that really help me. If you want peace, you need to be connected with God through praying and reading his Word. I mention verses from the book of Psalms, but because they're so many, I encourage you to read through Psalms yourself. Again, if you are not saved, you are not a child of God. If you choose to reject Jesus as your Lord and savior, you forfeit many of God's promises.

1 Peter 5:7

Casting all your care [anxiety] upon him; for he careth for you.

Philippians 4:6–7

Be careful [anxious] for nothing; but in every thing by prayer and supplication with thanksgiving let your requests be made known unto God. And the peace of God, which passeth all understanding, shall keep your hearts and minds through Christ Jesus.

Luke 12:6–7

Are not five sparrows sold for two farthings, and not one of them is forgotten before God? But even the very hairs of your head are all numbered. Fear not therefore: ye are of more value than many sparrows.

Isaiah 66:13

As one whom his mother comforteth, so will I comfort you.

Isaiah 51:12–13

I, even I, am he that comforteth you: who art thou, that thou shouldest be afraid of a man that shall die, and of the son of man which shall be made as grass; And forgettest the Lord thy maker, that hath stretched forth the heavens, and laid the foundations of the earth.

Isaiah 49:16

Behold, I have graven thee upon the palms of my hands.

Isaiah 46:4

And even to your old age I am he; and even to hoar hairs will I carry you: I have made, and I will bear; even I will carry, and will deliver you.

How to Be Saved

First of all, what are we to be saved from? The answer: from our sins.

What is sin? It's breaking *any* of God's rules or falling short of perfection. God is holy and cannot be in the presence of sin. However, he loves us and wants us to fellowship with him and to love him by our own free will, and therefore he gives us free choice. Because of this, we have the freedom to do good or evil, which is clearly seen by looking at the rates of crime, murder, and rape in this world. In fact, death and suffering itself is a result of sin. "For the wages of sin is death; but the gift of God is eternal life through Jesus Christ our Lord" (Romans 6:23).

Did you catch that? "But the gift of God is eternal life through Jesus Christ our Lord."

God's one and only son, Jesus Christ himself, paid for each and every one of our sins by shedding his blood for us. He bled and died and was raised to life again three days later, therefore completely paying our debt and allowing us to live in the presence of God in heaven—but we must receive it. If you refuse what God did for us, you have to pay for your sins yourself, which is not only the death of your body but your soul into hell forever. The truth is we can never pay for our sins before an eternal holy God. This is why it is so important to receive God's free gift.

So how do you receive this gift of eternal life? Admit you are a sinner needing saved. The Bible says, "For all have sinned, and come short of the glory of God" (Romans 3:23).

Believe and confess. The Bible says "that if thou shalt confess with thy mouth the Lord Jesus, and shalt believe in thine heart that God hath raised him from the dead, thou shalt be saved" (Romans 10:9).

CPSIA information can be obtained
at www.ICGtesting.com
Printed in the USA
LVHW101532131121
703253LV00004B/133